THE BEGINNING

I was born on April 27, 1967 in a hospital at South Williamson Kentucky, across the river from a small town called Williamson West Virginia. Williamson is the largest city in Mingo County along the Tug River Valley. A population of 3000 it was known for its railway hub that connected to the coal mines in the area.

My mother, Barbara, was only 19 years old when she had me. My mother was a Virgo and she fit the profile perfectly. She was very outgoing and loved life. She partied all of her life and had hundreds of friends who loved her. She was beautiful and sexy and she knew it. She was a professional model for several years and men were crazy about her everywhere she went. She was too young to have a kid but it happened. Eventually she would have 3 kids, my half brother Anthony and my sisters Taryn and Ashley. My father left her when she told him she was pregnant. For the majority of my life I never knew who my father was and referred to my grandfather as dad.

I was raised by my grandparents, Eugene and Norma Thorn, and I was given the last name Thorn instead of my father's last name. In my entire life I only saw my real father twice and had no relationship with him in any way. It never bothered me that I did not really know this man, I just did not think about it.

My mother married a guy named Leon Heard when I was 10 years old. He was a Lawyer and owned a travel agency in Cleveland. He had a successful law practice due to his tenacious fighting for his clients. He was a really good stepfather and he and I got along well. He was a loud and boisterous character who truly loved my

1

mother.

My grandparents were wonderful people, my grandmother was a devout Christian who worked sometimes as a cook at the local Piggly Wiggly, but mostly was a homemaker. She made me go to Sunday school every week and church as much as she could.

I think she is the reason I did not remain very religious as I grew older. I had enough religion growing up. She was a really nice lady but she could be tough if you wronged her in any way. When she loved you she would do anything for you and she really loved me.

My grandfather worked in the coal mines and was a strong parent who took care of his family. He was an amazing guy because he good do any trade you could think of, he just knew how to do it. He was very funny and loved to tell stories. He was liked by everybody and if you went anywhere with him be prepared for people to come up and talk to him. He and my grandmother had 5 kids besides my mother so I had plenty of aunts and uncles in the house as I grew up.

Eventually my mother left me with my grandparents and she moved to Cleveland to pursue a career in modeling. She loved me but was not ready to take care of a kid and try to pursue her dream to become a model.

Williamson was a normal small town in coal country where the best jobs were coal mines and the railroad, like many towns in West Virginia at that time. I had a great childhood there and ex-celled in school and athletics. I was good in football, baseball and especially basketball from a very young age.

HIGH SCHOOL

I had a normal education and was an honor society member and I graduated from Williamson High School with honors near the top of my class. I was in a gifted class throughout high school with about 12 other kids. We competed very hard with each other in our college prep classes. When I got to high school I focused on basketball and I began to build a reputation in the state as one of the best players.

I played on some championships teams and as a freshman played on a nationally ranked team with Mark Pine, an All American and one of the top players in the country.

As I got closer to graduation I began to receive letters from colleges across the country. My junior and senior year I was named All State as a top player in the state of West Virginia.

At home I was a good kid, and was raised with manners and strict rules of behavior due to my grandmother. I had many friends,and girlfriends and almost never got into trouble. When I did get into trouble I was punished with a belt or a switch as my grandparents believed in this kind of punishment. If I ever acted up my grandmother would threaten to tell my grandfather and I would immediately act better. I was afraid of my grandfather when it came to punishment, even though he loved me like a son. They also pushed school as important at a young age and I kept that attitude all through each level of my education.

School came easy to me and I mostly made straight A's and won many awards over the years. I was also into computers when I was like ten years old. I was so good that I was writing my own programs. For most of my early life I wanted to go into computer science when I went to college but later I changed my goal to engineering.

High School was the best time as I was a basketball star and a good student so I was very popular with teachers and students. However as a sophomore something happened that would change my life.

My girlfriend my sophomore year was Kathy Hatcher, a girl I met from an older friend of mine. She got pregnant and I broke up with her almost immediately.

Her response was to decide to have the baby since she could not have me. One day out of the blue she came to the house with the baby and my grandfather tracked me down and made me come home to see my new son Jonathan. I was crushed, I thought my basketball future was over because of this baby. I tried to deny he was my kid, but he looked just like me even as a baby.

I was too young to be a father and I refused to be a part of his life, so I could move on with my life.

My junior year was much better because Kathy left school for awhile and everyone kind of forgot about the matter. My grandfather never let me forget but I was able to move on.Looking back on it I did exactly what my father had done.

Baseketball was my outlet, for any problem that I had in school. I was one of the best players in the State and I knew it. I was becoming more and more conceited as my name and picture was in the local newspaper almost every other day. By the time I was a senior I knew I was going to get a full scholarship offer from somebody.

I was having a great year and the team was headed to the West Virginia State Tournament thus creating even more exposure for me. In the end I chose a scholarship to West Virginia Tech, which was known as a small engineering school in Montgomery, West

Virginia.

COLLEGE

After graduating and arriving at college I moved into an apartment with two other teammates. Montgomery is a small town near Charleston West Virginia but there is nothing there except for the school. I knew after my first month there this was not where I wanted to be. I was bored and although my roommates were good guys I still hated being there. I had signed a full scholarship, so I had a free ride, everything was paid for and my only worry was studying and playing ball. On my first visit home I told my grandfather I was going to leave and apply to West Virginia University (WVU). He was furious but he just did not understand. I knew I would be accepted at WVU because of my excellent grades and school honors.My grandfather told me if I left he would not give me any financial support. I did not care I had been to Morgantown a few times and really liked the WVU campus. WV Tech did not have a campus, it was just a small town with a school on a few streets. WVU was a decent sized University with over 30,000 students and is known nationally as a football school.The school offered many types of undergraduate and graduate academic programs.

I applied immediately and just prior to the holidays I was accepted, so I made my decision and when I came home for the holiday break I did not go back to WV Tech.

WEST VIRGINIA UNIVERSITY

My grandfather and I argued almost the entire holiday vacation but my mind was made up and I had planned on getting financial aid and loans to pay for a transfer to WVU. Many of my former high school classmates went to WVU so I had no problem getting a ride to Morgantown after the new year.

I enrolled and started classes at WVU in the new year. My plan was to tryout for the basketball team the following year since it was already too late to do so this year. I was finally happy and really enjoyed being at WVU with many of my former friends from Williamson.

I did ok at WVU but I really did not put in the effort I should have. I was always broke so things were really tough, especially my first year there. My grandfather kept his word about not helping me during my first year. Once he saw that I was determined to make it, he changed his mind and began to help financially.

I was just studying enough to get by and was not really sure what I wanted to do, so I changed my major from engineering to liberal arts to business, I had no idea about my future. My grades were not very good because I was not really focused and I was not sure what career I wanted to pursue.

After my freshman year, I planned to tryout for the team. I had been playing with many of the WVU players in pick-up games in the summer and I knew I could play at that level. When the time came, I did not tryout and to this day I don't know why I made that decision. It was like one day I just woke up and decided my basketball career was over and it was time to plan for my future. I did research on numerous careers and decided I wanted to be a stockbroker.

The movie Wall Street had a profound effect on my decision. I use to watch that movie over and over just for motivation to go to class. I did this every day until I graduated.

I had only had a few girlfriends in college. My first year I was dating an old high school girlfriend. Amy Percy, on and off, until I met a girl named Chareen Rogers. We met one day by accident and began dating until we were seniors. We had some good times together and she had a really nice family. Later that year I met another girl name Durietha Dziorney, who lived at the same apartment complex and we had a couple of dates just prior to me leaving college.

She was also a student but was in another relationship at the time so things did not go too far but she would remained a part of my life forever. We will get to that later in the story. Although I graduated, I was unable to participate in the ceremony because I had so many parking tickets that I could not pay. The School refused to give me my diploma until the tickets were paid and it was years before I paid them back and got my diploma.

When it was time to leave school, I had decided that I wanted to live in Atlanta, I had visited there a few times and loved the city. From my research, I wanted to work for the biggest brokerage firm in the world, Merrill Lynch. The firm employed over 30,000 stockbrokers and had offices all over the world.

I applied for a job in the Atlanta Office and packed my car for the ride to Atlanta for my first interview.

My grandfather helped me get a car for my birthday earlier in the year, a used BMW and I loaded everything I had into that car and hit the road.

WALL ST. DREAMS

Once I got to Atlanta I moved into a Motel 6 and prepared for my interview. I had one suit and two shirts to my name. I had about one thousand dollars and and a car full of stuff I could not move into the room, it was like an adventure. I survived two rounds of interviews from several candidates and by the third interview I felt like I was going to get the job. After my third interview I was told I made the final round and there were three candidates left but they were going to hold off hiring anyone at this time due to the war in the gulf that had just started. This delay would be a few weeks to a few months, and unfortunately I could not afford to stay in a motel that long. I was running out of money and did not know what to do. I called my mother in Cleveland and told her my situation and she said I could come there if I needed somewhere to go. I waited a few more days and made the decision to give up my dream of living in Atlanta, I packed up and headed north. I drove to Raleigh, North Carolina and stopped in to visit my old girlfriend Chareen who now lived there with her family. I stayed there for a few weeks, checking in on the Merrill Lynch job until there was still no decision made so I had to choose between staying there and trying to build a future with Chareen or leaving and heading to Cleveland. In the end I chose to leave and drove to Cleveland and moved in with my mother, stepfather, and two younger sisters, Taryn and Ashley.

WALL ST. CAREER

After settling in Cleveland, I reapplied to Merrill Lynch via the Cleveland office and after a few months I got an interview. I went through several rounds of interviews there and was hired by the sales manager, Doug Berger, along with two other guys on Sept.20, 1991. Merrill Lynch was everything I thought it would be and I was super excited with my new job. I got my first paycheck and moved out of my parents house into a new apartment on my own. My starting salary was #$40,000 and basically all I did was prepare for the Series 7 securities exam.

The downtown Cleveland office was huge with about one hundred and fifty brokers and did tremendous business for Merrill Lynch. The broker's in the downtown, east and west offices managed hundreds of millions of dollars in assets and it would surprise many people how wealthy the Cleveland area really is.

The office was very nice with mahogany everywhere, museum quality pictures on the walls and views of downtown Cleveland and Lake Erie. I could not believe how many millionaires were in that office and I made it my goal to get to know all of them and learn as much as I could from each of them. The office was laid out cubicle style and each desk had a Quotron computer on it.
An outer perimeter of private offices were reserved for the big producers. After my first week there I made it my goal to earn one of those private offices.

Merrill Lynch had a unique training system where new brokers or Financial Consultants as brokers are called at Merrill Lynch are partnered with a senior broker for the first year or two as a mentor. My mentor was a twenty year broker named Bill Sholem, an older Lebanese guy who did around $800,000 in production. This means commissions as brokers are paid about thirty five percent of their gross production. So Bill earned about $300.000 per year and made it look so easy sitting in his big office overlooking lake Erie.

I was in heaven, it was better than anything I had imagined. Money was everywhere in that office, you could smell it, and all I had to do was pass the securities exam and get to work to get my share.

I studied all day every day and in the evening, the firm provided food for anyone working late, so I saved a lot of money on dinners. Whenever I took a break from studying, I would walk around the offices which was actually two floors in this building, watching the brokers. I wanted to be just like them in every way. I quickly realized I had to work on my wardrobe, I was rotating two shirts with my one suit. I also paid attention to the shoes which were expensive and always polished.

There was a guy in the office named Charlie, who would shine shoes during the day.

I happened to be walking around downtown Cleveland one day at lunch and went into a suit store and met the owner. A nice arab guy who had recently opened this store and was eager for customers. His name was Muhammed and he and I hit it off right away and he made me the best deal ever. He let me pick out six suits, shirts and ties and he would allow me to make payments for them since I was a new broker and could not afford this at once. His only condition was that I send other brokers in the office to him for some business. He and I became friends over the years and I bought twenty suits and shirts from him during my career.

I was now ready for my journey into a Wall Street career. Branch offices like mine were all connected to the main headquarters on Wall Street, so you always felt like you were right there in New

York. There are squawk boxes or speakers all over the office with the firms analysts in New York providing information all day.

The day of my Series 7 test, I was so nervous that I could barely walk into the testing center. After several hours I finished the test and was told that I passed but not actually what I scored. So when the lady said I passed I was so excited I headed straight for Tiffany's; my favorite gentlemans club, to celebrate. I was now a stockbroker just like Bud Fox from the Wall Street movie. I was given my production number the following week and a cubicle near Bill's office. My production number is how the firm would know to pay me for any trades that I did. There were vacuum tubes built into the walls all around the office where you would write a trading ticket and then shoot it through the tubes directly to the wire room which connected directly to the exchanges on Wall Street in New York.

Bill and I shared his secretary, Denise who had worked with him for years. Denise was black which was nice since there were only two blacks in the entire office other than me. One was a broker named Byron, he was really cool and helped me during my first few months.

I started doing what every new broker does to find clients, cold calling, and I dialed for hours everyday until I started opening accounts. It was great because if I needed help I could go to Bill anytime I wanted assistance in bringing in accounts. Bill was amazing, and he had a unique style of doing business. He arrived very early in the morning and sold a lot of fixed income products like bonds. He would be on the phone for a few hours and get his daily production goal finished before noon. He would go for a walk to smoke and then come back and do more business until around 2pm and he was done for the day. He made it look so easy, he had about eighty million dollars in assets under management so he had a very nice book of clients.

As a rookie financial consultant at Merrill Lynch you had goals in order to be recognized by the firm as first quintile. This means you rank worldwide among Merrill brokers at the top of your class based on your (LOS) length of service. You had to have 100 accounts with $10 Million in accounts under management in your first year.

This was the goal of every new broker and it was not an easy achievement. If you met that goal you earned a bonus and a trip to the Merrill Lynch campus in Princeton New Jersey for advanced training. This was all apart of the PDP or Professional Development Program.
You need to open about ten accounts per month to track this goal so there was no time to waste. My Sales Manager Doug Berger would invite anyone who opened ten accounts in the month to a fancy dinner at a popular Cleveland restaurant. I worked my ass off to win these dinners as well as any Merrill sponsored trips. These were all expense paid trips around the world and were available to anyone who achieved certain goals.

During my career I went on amazing trips to Vegas, Bermuda, Jamaica, and New Orleans just to name a few. The Merrill Lynch trips were first class.

I remember the New Orleans trip we were in a huge banquet hall about to have dinner when all of a sudden a huge Mardi Gra parade came marching through the building. It was incredible with high school bands, floats, and dancers. Another amazing trip was to Bermuda and Castle Harbour Hotel. A beautiful hotel on a cliff overlooking the ocean, The beaches in Bermuda have pink sand and we had a buffet dinner one evening on the beach.

I loved it here and I met some real characters inat office. Guys like Lee Chen, a Chinese broker who was really funny and would walk around the office in slippers while he produced over eight hundred thousand. Stuart Bertman, who was a Rabbi and a million dollar producer. Paul Satez, another million dollar producer who was almost never in the office because he did his business in lunch meetings with his clients. Vince Tanzo, a young second year broker who was already doing about four hundred thousand in production. He and Bill Toms another rookie were the young rising stars in the office. Every firm has a big swinging dick, the top producer and in our office that was Lou Tambino, a short italian guy who did about three million in production and had a wing in the building all to himself. He had three secretaries who split the alphabet of his clients. Lou was the man, when he walked to the restroom brokers would notice. Every so often our Sales Manager Doug would have Lou come and talk to the newer brokers about what it took to be like him.

Those were great speeches, the guy was a machine and I was in awe. I would ask some of the older brokers who started with Lou what he was like as a rookie and the response from all of them was that he never put the phone down, he smiled and dialed all day long. One of my closest friends was Mike Zeger, the nephew of legendary investor Martin Zeger. He was a young guy doing about three hundred thousand in production. He loved trading stocks and was instrumental in helping me develop a love for trading stocks during my career. I was later amazed at how little education was dedicated to the art of picking stocks.

As Merrill brokers we had received the best training on Wall Street yet none of it was how to buy stocks. As far as Merrill Lynch was concerned that was not really our job. Our job was to bring in assets under management and generate commissions from those assets by selling financial products, not just sitting in the office buying and selling stocks. This was the difference between Merrill Lynch and all the other Wall Street firms.

One day after about eight months in the business, I was called into my manager's office and told I was invited to go to Princeton as I was on track to meet the PDP goals. I was so excited as I had heard so much about this trip helping guys do better when they came back from this trip. When my time came I flew to Newark and was pick-up by a limo driver at the airport and driven to a beautiful campus in Princeton New Jersey.

The property was like a college campus and one of the buildings was a hotel. The trip was a one week training at Merrill's facilities, where most of their analysts were located. Each day we had meetings and presentations from some of the top brokers within Merrill Lynch from across the country. They told us exactly how they did business, how they prospected for clients or marketed themselves. We learned the best techniques for building a business to become a million dollar producer.

There was also restaurants at the property which allowed you to meet and have dinner with other brokers and share ideas. When I returned back to Cleveland I was so much more confident and motivated to take my business to the next level.

The goal of graduating from PDP became more meaningful after learning that I would earn a $100,000 dollar bonus that vested in 10 years just for finishing the program and staying with the firm for 10 years. I completed the program by the end of that year and was on my way to building a solid business. I met another broker named Frank who did about six hundred thousand loved trading stocks.

He showed me a few tricks that would help me do more business. Merrill Lynch was a market maker in many stocks and by hitting a few keys on the keyboard of the quotron computer you could find out if any stock was a stock that we made a market in. Frank taught me how to bulk trade in those stocks and charge a quarter point commission buying and selling those stocks.

This changed my business in so many ways that I knew I wanted to develop clients that wanted to trade stocks. Over the next few years I focused on finding these types of clients and my production grew year to year.

I was making very good money for my age, My first year I

made $40,000, year two $80.000 and by my third year I made $120,000. I was rewarded with a private office and became one of the youngest brokers to get a private office. To help grow my business I started an internship program and hired a kid from college named Dave Trende. He would cold call for me in the evenings and help me open new accounts. Dave and I became really good friends over the years and when he finished college I gave him a referral to become a stockbroker himself. My business and income continued to grow year after year and by year six things really changed.

DEAN WITTER

A good friend name Rick Maz who was also a broker decided to leave Merrill and take a job as a Sales Manager at Dean Witter. Rick immediately started to try and recruit me and other young brokers. In this business recruiting brokers is a big business involving huge signing bonuses. Although I was making six figures Rick offered me $200,000 as a signing bonus if I left Merrill and came to Dean Witter. I loved Merrill and could never imagine leaving and working at another firm. Rick tried all year long to get me to leave, and only upfront cash kept me interested. When the offer hit $300,000 I started to seriously consider it. I agreed to meet with his bosses in Cleveland and Chicago and things went really well. They wanted me and offered additional incentives to lure me away. This is a big deal in the industry often leading to lawsuits,restraining orders, and settlements. When I finally decided to leave I had to start doing things to get ready for the date I was expected to resign.

First Dean Witter sent a guy to my office acting like a client to get a copy of my clients statements so they could copy them and prepare letters. This is standard practice but was very nerve racking because you really can't tell clients what your planning for fear they might tell your manager. These clandestine things went on for about a month until the day came when I was told to wait until 4pm. I was told to walk in and resign to the senior manager at Merrill at that time because it would be to late in the day for them to go to court and get a restraining order. Letters would be mailed to my clients along with transfer papers for them to transfer their account with me to Dean Witter.

At 4:10 on a friday afternoon, I nervously walked from my office to David Rucks office and he was on the phone so I had to wait a minute. The whole time I stood their thinking he already knows that I am leaving and he is on the phone with the firms lawyers right now. His secretary told me to go in and I walked in and told him I was resigning from the firm and I quickly walked out of the office to the elevators. I had already taken my personal things from my office over the past month. I got down to the buildings lobby and Rick was there waiting for me.

We walked across the street to Dean Witters building and when I got to their office they immediately had me sign a contract and handed me a certified check for $250,000.

They walked me around the office and took me to my new office which was huge and overlooked the city and lake Erie. It was an incredible view and they introduced me to my new secretary a girl named Tonya who was very attractive. I immediately started to call my best clients and explain things and tried to get them to transfer their accounts. Many of them had already been called by Merrill Lynch brokers that quick.

Things were not going too well because Tonya was new and learning their systems, so over the next few weeks transfers were getting screwed up and clients were not happy about not knowing where their accounts were between the two firms. Part of my deal was to be paid a guaranteed salary of $15,000 per month for six months until I could start generating commissions.

The following Monday, Merrill Lynch filed a lawsuit in court and was granted a temporary restraining order against me talking to my clients. Fortunately I had already contacted everyone of them and informed them that other Merrill brokers would call and try to get them to stay. This legal battle lasted for two weeks until the firms reached a settlement.I tried to get my business back on track with the clients that agreed to transfer. It was really a disaster the number of transfers that were not handled . If that was not bad enough I also quickly realized that Dean Witter did not make a market in stocks the way Merrill Lynch did so my business would dramatically have to change.

I was financially loaded but my business took a major hit and I knew I had made a major mistake by leaving. Over the next few months things got worse because many clients that transferred were not happy with the Dean Witter accounts and differences from Merrill.

Things hit rock bottom about six months later when one of my clients from Germany had many problems with his transfer and then the first few trades we made at Dean Witter all lost money and he had enough. Reinhold Schul was a friend of my uncle who lived in Germany and that is how I got his account. Without my knowledge he called Dean Witter headquarters and complained they had stole his money when they transferred his accounts.

None of this was true but he was acting like he had no idea what was going on and claimed he did not give me the ok to buy stocks in his new account. He was threatening lawsuits and acting really crazy.

My sales manager called me into the office one day and told me all of this went above him to his boss and that the firm had decided without hearing my side of the story to give him his money back and fire me. I almost had a heart attack standing there in his office when he said fire me. The only thing I thought to say was I was not giving the money back. The sales manager was just as upset as I was but said the decision was made by his bosses so he could not fix it.

The client had scared the shit out of everyone in Chicago headquarters with his erratic behaviour and they were certain he would create a scandal. I went home that day and cried, I had ruined my career by leaving Merrill and now six months later I was completely out of the business. I had just purchased my first home, a two bedroom three level townhouse in Ohio City and I was lost. I was facing a lawsuit from Dean Witter to recover their signing bonus and I was out of a job. Emotionally I was down and out and did not know what to do. A friend of mine John Mckinney tried to talk me into joining him to start a business but I said no.

It took about three months but I finally reached a settlement with Dean Witter for only $15,000 and that part of my life was over. I considered joining another brokerage firm but decided it was time to start my own business.

John had told me about an investment popular in Europe called bank debenture trading programs. I had never heard of it and began to do some research to find out if it was real. The investment returns were too hard to believe but the process sounded legitimate. There was a lot of secrecy around this investment because it was done using private placements. These are private transactions involving a small number of qualified investors and private banks. John did not have a source for the investment but was pursuing it nevertheless.

I figured I could find a source faster and began to search the internet. The limited information online involved a lot of warnings from the US government that this business did not exist.

TRADING PROGRAMS

The story goes that after World War II the nations of the world had a meeting at the Bretton Woods Conference in New York. The purpose of the meeting was to determine how to pay for the recovery and rebuilding of all of the destroyed cities in Europe from World War II. They decided to create a super safe investment that would attract private investment money into a bank controlled investment vehicle that paid an above average return.

Through this vehicle they would fund projects through the Bank for Reconstruction and Development and the IMF that would rebuild Europe and create humanitarian benefits. There were many names for this business, bank debenture trading, forfait financing, MTN trading etc. The process was simple a European bank would offer a Medium Term Note at a deep discount in which a private trader would purchase using private investor money. This trader would turn around and sell this note to an exit buyer at a premium and thus earn a profit. The trader would do this over and over in the course of a month until generating a substantial investment return for his private clients.

This business was regulated by the Federal Reserve and only available to investors with a minimum of $10 Million of private money. Because it was a business involving banks it was not regulated by the Securities Exchange Commission.

This would become an important fact in my life later. I decided I would try and find one of these traders so I began to travel around to meet people who were claiming they had access to these traders. According to research there were only 30 of these traders in the world but they did not solicit investors openly.

This effort was much more difficult than expected but after meeting a lot of phony people claiming to have access to a real trader in this business. I eventually met a guy from British Columbia named Dr. Subramanian, he was a retired banker who worked for Credit Suisse in London. He new everything about this business and still had a relationship with a trader.

The only issue was I did not have a minimum of $10 Million to invest. A guy I met during my search named Bill Ripp introduced Dr. Subramanian to me and I explained that me and my friends did not have that much available at this time. He suggested we find a trader that would take smaller amounts and pool with other investors, and he knew of a guy in Las Vegas doing deals for a minim of $100,000. So we set up a meeting with this guy Tony Rino who was pooling funds together for access to his trader in Belgium. Tony was offering 70 percent returns per month. I formed a new company called Global Investors Group (GIG) and put together a small group of friends and we pooled together $300,000 and off to Las Vegas I went with Bill Ripp. We met at Rino's home and signed a contract. He was a little Italian guy about 65 years old who had accidentally found out about this business and set up an operation with his bank, Norwest Bank in Vegas. He would pool monies together until he had $10 million and then go to his trader for a contract. He was offering 70 percent which meant he was earning twice that amount.

According to the contract we had to wait sixty days for our first payment and in a few months we got the wire transfer payment. I started to build GIG into more and more investors until I had $500,000 available for another deal. Unfortunately Rino was starting to have problems with the SEC (Securities Exchange Commission). They wanted him to stop pooling investor funds since he was not a registered rep.

In the end another bad thing happened to Rino. Norwest bank was sold, purchased by another bank in Vegas and they refused to continue managing Rino's operation. After about 3 payments Rino issued a letter explaining what had happened and suspending the program until he replaced his bank.

Eventually he setup his operation in Costa Rica in order to get away from the jurisdiction of the SEC. Ripp and I flew down to San Jose, Costa Rica to meet with Rino. Costa Rica was very third world it was so crowded downtown it was like New York. It was so much more dirty and gritty. We were taken to a law firm to set up companies registered in Costa Rica and then to Banco Del Pacifico in order to open accounts for these companies. It cost me $15,000 to set up these accounts

I set up three companies, one to make deposits, one as a holding company and one for distributions and then went to meet Rino.

He had a house set up in a compound with a gate and there was a line of people outside the house waiting to get in to see him. We were escorted in front of everyone and sat down with him to discuss our payments. We were assured payments would resume next month and that we would not have any more problems with distribution. I decided to go ahead and invest in another contract for $500,000 again at 70 percent per month. Payments started a few months later and everything was back on track. Things worked great and all I did was send a payment list to the bank and they sent out wire transfers to my clients in the US.

By the end of the 10 months GIG had made over $6.4 Million. I immediately re-invested for another contract. I was finally making some good money around 30% or $1.9 Million and it was time to really build this business.

MILLIONAIRE

I also felt it was time to start spending some money so I leased a beautiful 600 SL Mercedes convertible, and a BMW truck and purchased a mansion in Brecksville Ohio. An 8000 square foot house with 21 rooms and an elevator inside. The house was beautiful and I spent 200,000 decorating the house until I had it perfect. I built a theatre room, a game room, and workout room on the 2nd floor.

Life was good and I was ready to settle down from the constant working and trips that I had been doing for the past year.

My girlfriend Durietha and I were taking incredible vacations around the world and having fun. We use to go to the Bahamas in the winter, and take a cruise to the caribbean in the spring. In the summer we would go to LA for four days and stay in Santa Monica. We would rent a car and run all over the Hollywood Hills and Beverly Hills. We would spend all day sightseeing at Venice beach and Third Street Promenade then we would fly over to Vegas for three days. We would go to a few Vegas shows and sometimes rent a fancy sports car and take long drives in the desert. In September we always went to New York for a week and acted like real tourists visiting everything the city had to offer. Dinners every night in Little Italy and museums during the day. We had some really good times.

My friend Rick Maz and I moved to Miami for the winter. We rented a beautiful 3 bedroom apartment on Ocean Drive with an amazing view of the beach and the ocean. The apartment did not have walls it had a panoramic view of the beach and ocean the entire length of the apartment. I used to lay in my bedroom and look out at cruise ships heading out in the ocean. We played golf every morning and went out every night. We stayed in Florida until April and then we came back to Cleveland. Over the next few months we were going back and forth to Vegas every weekend. We golfed all day and hit the strip clubs at night spending a small fortune. I was having fun and trying to get the single life out of my system. I had made a decision that I was going to ask my girlfriend to marry me. One weekend my girlfriend and I flew to Chicago for the weekend and went to Cartier to pick out a ring. I asked her to marry me and brought her a $60,000 dollar 4 carat ring. I had become a millionaire in less than 2 years after losing my job and I wanted more.

I started to set up a network of agents across the country and later around the world. Each agent pooled a minimum of $1,000,000 of investor funds from their contacts and then brought those funds to Global Investors Group for a contract. GIG would then sign a master contract with a trading group and distribute payments.
I did a few more deals with Rino and then a deal with a guy named Terry Trepont representing a Spanish Foundation from Switzerland for $5 million.

My friend Derrick Kinney and I flew to Zurich. It was winter in Switzerland and it was a beautiful city. I could not believe I was walking down Bahnhofstrasse street looking at 500 year old banks. I opened an account at ABN AMRO bank one of the oldest banks in Europe. Trepnt offered me a contract that should have paid 300% over 10 months. Instead we only made 30% on that deal due to a bunch of excuses. I was so upset I had wasted 10 months on that deal. I actually think he did his deal but decided no to pay me.
As I was building this business, I was constantly trying to find a more direct trading source other than Rino because I did not want to keep sending him money and I did not want to travel back to

third world Costa Rica.

I had agents everywhere, Derrick Kinney, a good friend and stockbroker from Columbus Ohio. Ann Foster, a highly respected accountant in her community in New York. Bradford Wirter, an oil and gas entrepreneur from California. Renee Sorea computer executive in Maryland. Jim Spence an entrepreneur in Atlanta, Rick Maz my stockbroker friend who now lived in Chicago.

Dr Carl Jack a surgeon in Cleveland and Dr. Fred Harrison a internal medicine Doctor who owned a couple of diabetic clinics in Cleveland. I had Roger Weizen, a chef from Switzerland who spoke 7 languages and knew a lot of wealthy people in Europe. Dave my intern from Merrill Lynch also became an agent. In the end I would have 19 agents each participating with a minimum investment of $1 million to $8 million or more.

As I was building this group, Dr. Subramanian's trader past away from cancer and I was forced to find another trader. He introduced me to another trader at a company called Crane Limited.

This trader would only accept $100 Million clients so that was not an option but he introduced me to another guy who would take smaller amounts. His name was Stuart Rosen, and I spoke to him a few times before I had a $10 Million block ready to go. It was around this time that I decided I would try and build as big a block as I could. I had an idea to create a facility at a bank so Dr. Subramanian Introduced me to a banker at Bank One in Columbus. I met this banker and his boss and came up with a system of aggregated accounts that would pool up to a master account. The bank would give me a proof of funds for the total of all of these aggregated accounts.

This would allow me to pitch that each investor would have their own account at the bank and their funds would never leave their account. I would be able to get credit for the total amount to invest with a trader. This was incredible and made it hard to say no to this opportunity. Once this arrangement was set up I pitched it to my investor agents and we began to refer investors to the bank. We set up a minimum of $1 million to get an account and we were signing up people like crazy until word got out and strangers started calling the bank asking questions. People were calling me from all over the world. I had to stop it because we could not have strangers calling and exposing things.

When I finally shut it down we had $40 Million deposited at Bank One. Stuart Rosen offered a contract from his company RBP Financial for a 60/40 split of best effort trading per month up to 100% per quarter.

I signed the contract and shortly thereafter Stuart headed to London to set up the trade. He accepted a facility with Merrill Lynch London and a trading date was to start after the Holidays. This deal was going to be a game changer for me and my group. GiG would earn 40 percent off the top from this trade and we would pay our clients 70 percent of our profit. Expecting a non-guaranteed return of 100% per quarter GIG would earn 40 percent of $160 Million or $64 Million dollars. I would earn 30 percent of that for GIG or $19.2 Million and pay out $44.8 million to our clients.

I figured I could do at least one of these every 6 months until GIG had its own $100 Million to invest without any client funds. This was the plan and the long term goal was to set up my own venture capital firm.

THE DEAL

After the holidays we began to set up for the transaction. I instructed my banker to have Bank One to talk Bank to Bank with Merrill Lynch London, Rosen's Bank to set up authentication via Swift or KTT, which is how banks communicate. The banks worked out these keys and set a date for delivery. The plan was that Bank One would send a KTT for our $40 Million to Merrill London and Merrill London would authenticate via the key codes they had arranged. Then Bank One would delivery a hard copy of the facility with two bank officer signatures.

Once Marrill received this document and everything was verified they would release trading funds to RBP to begin trading.

I got an early morning call from Stuart, telling me we had a problem. Apparently Merrill London received the document and then went to Bank One London to authenticate the signatures of the two bank officers. Bank One London refused to authenticate and instead called Scotland Yard. Stuart was beside himself angry. I had no idea what to do since I had no idea what the hell he was talking about. Scotland Yard is like the FBI in America. He instructed me to call my banker and find out what was going on.

I called my banker Craig Morton and he told me that Scotland Yard has been on the phone with his bosses at headquarters in Chicago and that he was waiting on a call from the legal department to find out what happened.

I relayed this information to Stuart in London and we waited to find out what was going on. This went on for days and still no information came from my banker. Stuart decided he could not stay in London any longer so he returned home to California. After a few days I could not get my banker on the phone and I left numerous messages, as Stuart was all over me about what was happening.

Then one day I get Federal Express package from the Securities Exchange Commission with a subpoena for records from the Chicago office. The SEC regulates all securities transactions in the United States for the Federal Government. I informed Stuart and he told me I better get a securities lawyer on retainer and respond to the subpoena.

I was losing my mind since I had no idea what the hell was happening. Again I was having a hard time reaching my banker and finally I complained to his secretary and she finally had a lawyer from the bank call me back to tell me that he had been terminated. When I asked why I was told Bank Fraud.The Lawyer was being very secretive about what happened.

I relayed this information to Stuart and he told me that if I could move my funds to another bank we could probably still complete the transaction. So I decided to go to my other bank Key Bank and see if they could mirror the setup we had at Bank One. After a meeting they were eager to set up the same account system called Zero Balance accounts.

I notified the clients what was happening and everyone voted to move the money. We arranged for packets of account paperwork to be sent to everyone and had them send in withdrawal requests to Bank One. After a week or so we got the accounts set up at the new bank and waited for the monies to be transfered. Another week went by and nothing happened. Nobody had their money transferred and when they called Bank One they could not get an answer why. Eventually Stuart and I called the bank and we were transferred to the legal department in Chicago. We were told the money was on hold because the bank did not know what was going on with the credit facility that was issued fraudulently.

We asked how was this fraud when you have our money backing up the facility. We were told one of the officer signatures was forged making the document fraudulent.

When I argued that had nothing to do with me and my money they responded they did not care until they knew what was going on with this facility. We were told no money would be transferred.

We threatened to sue and their response was we will see you in court. Stuart and I discussed what to do next. He decided he had to cancel the transaction and contemplated he may have to sue my company for the loss of profits The next day he called with more strange news.

One of his bank relationships in Germany had called him and sent him a copy of a SWIFT message that Bank One had sent out to every Bank in Europe that any bank receiving a credit facility from Bank One in the name of RBP Financial was fraudulent and should be returned to Bank One immediately. His banker thought this was very strange and amateurish. Stuart told me I needed to file a lawsuit against Bank One.

I went to our investors and told them what was happening and that the bank refused to release our money. Everyone agreed that we should retain a lawyer if I paid for it. One of my investors in California, a lawyer, recommended a law firm from Philadelphia with a reputation for suing banks. The firm was called Cozen & O'connor and I retained them immediately for $50,000. I had a conference with the firm's attorney and they filed a lawsuit in federal court in Columbus Ohio. I was told that I needed to hire another law firm to represent me personally separate from the investors. This costs me another $50,000.

A week later I get a frantic call from my new lawyer in Columbus that the SEC showed up in federal court today and asked the judge for a freeze on all of my personal assets. I was told that as of 12 noon today all of my bank accounts were now frozen. I immediately hung up the phone and jumped in my car and drove to the local ATM machine and withdrew the maximum from every bank account that I could.

I did not care if this violated a court order I was not going to be broke. With all of this going on I still had no idea of what really happened with the authentication of the document sent to London. Bank One's response to our lawsuit was to counter sue, in the suit they finally admitted what happened.

My banker Craig Morton forged the signature of the second officer on the document. This did not make any sense to me, why would he do that and more importantly how is that my fault. Craig Morton works for the bank therefore it's their responsibility if he did something wrong.

To make matters worse, Bank One called the SEC and acted as if they had no idea what we were doing and needed help stopping a fraud. Of course this was not true but it helped to muddy the waters for them. If they could put pressure on us then perhaps their fraud would be overlooked. We learned many interesting things when we started to depose their people.

We learned of this strategy and another strategy of trying to attack my investors. They ran background checks on each investor in my group hoping to find something dirty, yet everyone was clean which I already knew.

They transferred Morton's boss across the country to make it difficult to depose him since he was in the original meeting that I had with Morton to set things up. Their legal strategy was to try and act as if Morton and I were close partners and that he forged this document on my behalf. This was far from the truth, since I had no relationship with Morton other than Banker to client.

We finally got to depose Morton who admitted the only reason he forged the other banker's signature was because the guy was out of the office a few days and Morton did not want to delay the transaction. He had no idea he was making the situation worse and basically committed fraud when it was not necessary to do so.

These depositions went on for weeks and were digging a bigger and bigger hole for Bank One. On their side they simply sat back and allowed the SEC to do all of their dirty work.

THE GOVERNMENT

The SEC went after every investor forcing them to outline in detail how they made the money they invested and did they pay their taxes on that money. They went after me personally by accusing me of running a ponzi scheme. They also accused me of soliciting investment money without registering the investment with the SEC. This is securities fraud 101 but had nothing to do with my operation. Bank transactions are not under the jurisdiction of the SEC but their strategy was to ignore the actual transaction and focus on how I raised money. I had to travel to Chicago for a deposition with the SEC. I hired an SEC lawyer from Texas to meet me there.

We walked into this building into a huge dirty office filled with boxes everywhere for this deposition. Two young female SEC lawyers were there and they deposed me for 8 hours with the most ridiculous questions imaginable. They had no idea about my business and it was really a fishing expedition. When we left the lawyer told me to expect them to file a complaint against me in the next month and sure enough they did exactly that in Federal Court in Columbus Ohio. The complaint alleged that I was running a ponzi scheme and soliciting investors all over the United States. They alleged I was using the money for my personal use for my lavish lifestyle.

The next week I had a strategy session with my new attorney to discuss the case and the SEC complaint. My attorney asked two other lawyers in the firm to sit in on the meeting while I told my story. I later learned that the firm billed me for 3 lawyers and nearly depleted my retainer. I fired them immediately and a lawyer friend of the family told me that was something that lawyers do to make more money. A lesson I had to learn the hard way, and now I still needed a lawyer. The family friend was Steve Helfgott and he was a bankruptcy attorney so he could not help me but he would make a few calls for me.

I hired a guy named Bill Conner who was the head of the Bar Association in Columbus. We met and settled on a retainer of $25,000. We had a hearing coming up to discuss the asset freeze so things were moving quickly. Meanwhile I was receiving subpoenas from the SEC on a weekly basis for documents. This went on for months, as they definitely showed their subpoena power. They sent subpoenas to all of my banks scaring the shit out of them. The next week they all called to tell me I had a week to close my bank accounts.

The hearing was a disaster, somehow I wound up on the stand testifying in front of the Judge. It was not my best day and I was pissed my attorney let it happen. I knew I was in trouble and had to find a new bank even though my assets were frozen.
I still had bills to pay and a mortgage on my home. Fortunately I had $500,000 hidden in a Swiss account so I planned to wire that into a new bank. I set up an account with American Express Bank online, and wired the money from Amro Bank in Switzerland.

Once the money arrived I had $30,000 wired to my personal assistant Kim Edison and she had it converted to money orders that I could cash when I needed money. I hoped this would not leave a trail for the SEC.

The crazy thing was while all of this was going on I was about to get married to my girlfriend, Durietha Dziorney. We had decided to get married at Atlantis resort in the Bahamas.

This would cost me about $25,000. We decided to invite family and friends to the wedding and fly them to the Bahamas. I was in a world of trouble and most of my money was frozen but I could not tell her that we could not get married right now. Unknown to us at the time, Michael Jordan was hosting his annual golf tournament at the resort at the same time as our wedding. There were celebrities all over the resort during that week so all of my group had an amazing time and we had a wonderful wedding and honeymoon. I knew things were going to be crazy when we returned home but I had no idea how bad things would get.

While I was fighting the SEC my clients were still trying to get their money from Bank One. The law firm that I hired was doing a good job but they wanted more money and I could not afford to pay them.

Fortunately they convinced the clients to pay some money by convincing them they needed to separate themselves from me in the fight. My SEC issues were complicating things for them against Bank One. This worked out for me because I was no longer on the hook for the fees. Eventually our firm would win in a settlement and Bank One agreed to release the money with interest.

The day before the funds were to be released the SEC showed up in court and asked the Judge to freeze the funds and appoint a Receiver to make the disbursements. The government tricks were never ending in this matter.

Over the next year the Court Appointed Receiver, Michael Greedy, who we learned was a friend of the Judge. He billed from the investors money for his fees on average about $60,000 per month. He took his time investigating every client and how they acquired the money they had invested with me. In the end he only paid back about 70% of their money while making a small fortune for himself. Of course I was blamed for the difference even though I had not touched this money.

Meanwhile I had several 8 hour depositions with the SEC over the next few months. They even deposed my wife who knew nothing about my business. My attorney started to prepare for a trial by spending a lot of time at my home going over my story and looking at my documents.

He was burning through my retainer and wanting more money. I did not want to pay him from my secret account because I did not want the SEC to find out about it so I told him I had no more money other than what was frozen. He filed a motion with the Judge to get his fee from the frozen funds. The Judge agreed and he remained my attorney.

We prepared for months and after many hearings we finally had a trial date. My attorney believed my story and finally had a good handle on my case. He had spoken to my clients who all had good things to say about me and rejected the SEC accusations that I had defrauded them.

Early one morning I was awakened by my doorbell ringing over and over and then banging on my door. When I got to the front door there were 20 FBI agents at my door with a search warrant. I let hem in and they hurried all over my house. They took my computers and every document from my file cabinets. I was freaking out now, things were getting really serious. My wife had went to work early that morning and just missed the 10 cars in the driveway.

I called my attorney and he told me I was going to need a criminal attorney so he helped me meet with on of the top criminal attorneys in Cleveland, Roger Berg.

I met him and explained what happened. He contacted the prosecutor's office and discovered they were just getting started and no indictment was coming anytime soon. He was able to make arrangements to get my stuff back within a few days. At this point I was under so much stress and this was exactly what the Government wanted.

We were only a week or so away from our trial date and were meeting daily to prepare our defense strategy. Then it happened, I received a call from my attorney one evening and he told me the trial was vacated. The Judge had issued a summary judgement in favor of the SEC.

There would be no trial and the ruling was that I was liable for $7.4 million dollars and my assets were to be disgorged. I was shocked that they could cancel a trial and just give the Government a victory without proving anything. My attorney explained that this was a civil case not a criminal case so things worked differently.

The next week I get a visit from the Court Appointed Receiver who wants to come into my home with a camera crew to document my furniture and possessions.
He informed me that he was beginning the process of taking my home per the courts order to disgorge my assets. He informed me when the time came he would give me 30 days notice to vacate the property.

When my wife came home from work that evening I told her what had happened and about the FBI raid. I told her maybe it was time to get away from me because things were getting really bad. She then hit me with the final blow, she was pregnant. We just laid there on the bed and cried for hours. I did not know what I was going to do.

Fortunately for us the Receiver had a hard time taking our home. He did not have jurisdiction to just take our home and had to go through the proper legal channels which took months in the local courts. However he never left me alone, he showed up one day at our home to confiscate my wife's wedding ring which of course broke my wife's heart.

She had a $60,000 cartier diamond ring and all though I went and purchased her a new ring I could no longer afford a really expensive ring. He tried to take her mink coat and my watch collection but I refused and he left it alone for the time being. This type of harassment went on for most of that year. I was able to maintain my bills for a while but I was running out of money.

I decided the only thing to do was get back to work and try to do a deal with Rosen. I planned to find a single client with 100 Million that I could refer to Rosen and do a deal and make a commission to get on my feet. I had to be careful though because I could not let the SEC find out.

They must have expected me to do something like this because they started to wire tap my phones on certain days of the week. I had a close friend Dr. Subramanian who had a contact high up in the US Government who would check my phone and tell me when they were tapping my lines. You could hear the clicking sounds on the phone. I really did not have a choice, I had to make some money. Rosen agreed to continue to work with me despite what happened. I worked day and night trying to find a real client with that kind of money. I came across many phonies and wasted a lot of time with phone calls over the next few months to no avail.

Then our daughter Sabrina was born and we tried to be happy. I had stopped paying my mortgage and car payments and then the Receiver called to say he had finally got the authority to take my home and was willing to give me 90 days to leave since I had just had a new baby. This was a lie, he could not take my home because the bank owned it. He did however have two of my cars repossessed.

My wife was on leave from her job so we made the decision to leave in the next few months and move to her hometown in Wheeling WV.

We stayed in Wheeling for a few months and eventually moved to Florida. I had a friend Rick, who lived in Miami and was managing a recruiting firm and was willing to give me a job. We got settled in Weston Florida and began looking for jobs. Rick did not have an opening that paid a salary so I had to look for something else. My wife found a job in retail with Saks and I landed a job with a mortgage broker. We were doing ok for about six months and then I got a call from my stepfather.

My mom had died. We were in a Cheesecake factory when I got the call and I just broke down right there. I could not talk to tell my wife what was wrong. My mother had been battling a brain tumor for years and finally lost the battle. We went to the funeral and then decided to go to Wheeling for the holidays.

INDICTED

I went to visit my friend Derrick who was involved in the business and he gave me the bad news. We had been indicted and charged with Securities Fraud and Tax Evasion. I drove home that night and cried all the way home from Columbus. I knew we would have to leave Florida now and come back north in order to deal with these charges. We moved back to Wheeling and found an apartment.

I was notified in the mail that I had been indicted and was instructed to call Pretrial services. They asked me questions and verified my address and I had to explain we had just moved from Florida into a new apartment.
The arraignment was scheduled a week later and I did not have an attorney and could no longer afford one. They arranged a public defender named Sam Inez to meet me at the arraignment.

I drove myself to court that day and met Mr. Inez in the hall outside the courtroom. He knew nothing about my case and instructed me not to worry I would plead not guilty and bail would be set and I could go home. During the hearing the Judge asked pretrial services if they were recommending bail and they said not at this time.

They were unable to confirm my residence since I had just moved.

The Judge asked the prosecutor if they had an opinion on bail and they said that I had money all over the world and was a flight risk. He then asked me to respond. I told him I no longer had any money anywhere and I pulled out my passport and handed it to the clerk. The Judge thought for a minute and denied bail until my address could be confirmed. I was arrested right there in the courtroom and taken to a cell in the basement of the courthouse. I could not believe this was happening but things would only get worse.

I sat there for hours and after processing and fingerprinting me they handcuffed me again and took me to a car with two marshals sitting in the front seat.

CCA

The Marshals drove me from Akron to Youngstown and all I could think about was my car at the courthouse and the fact that my wife would have no idea where I was.

We arrived at a maximum security facility with gun towers and barb wire fences all around the facility. I was taken to a holding facility with about 50 guys sitting in a cage waiting to be given an orange uniform. After changing our clothes our property was bagged up and placed in storage lockers and we were taken to a medical area. We were given a medical check up and questioned about our medical past. We were then taken to a pod area, just like in the movie OZ.

I was scared to death as I looked through the door and could see inmates screaming and making noise in the pod. I was waiting to get assigned a room when a crazy looking guy looked at me through the door window and he licked the window while staring at me. I was taken to a room with two other inmates and shown a boat on the floor with a mat in the boat and told this was my bed for a few days. I asked if I could make a phone call and the guard pointed in the main room to a phone. I made a collect call to my wife and told her what happened. She immediately started crying and saying she could not take this anymore. I felt terrible but did not want these guys to see me crying. It was packed in this place and very loud. It had been a long day and I was exhausted. When I laid down in this boat my head was right under the toilet. I went to sleep I was so tired.

I was in this hell for 3 months. The food was terrible there were fights everyday and it was very dangerous place because it was violent inmates mixed with non violent inmates. It was called CCA and had a horrible reputation unknown to me. I did my best to stay out of the way until I was finally moved to another room and given a top bunk. We were locked down 23 hours per day and allowed to go outside for 1 hour per day. All you could do was watch TV, play cards or chess and read, that was it.

After a week the public defender came to see me and we talked about my case. I knew in 5 minutes I could not go to trial with this guy because he had no clue what securities fraud was. I met a guy after a few weeks that had a sentencing book and he taught me how the sentencing guidelines worked. We were able to calculate how much time I was facing based on my charges. I was facing 12 years for these charges mainly because of the amount of money involved in my case. I was fucked. His name was Tony and he had been to prison before for taxes and he explained to me that prison was 100 times better than this place. I could not relate to that at all, based on prison in the movies. He explained that I would go to a different kind of prison because I had no violence in my history and this was a first time offense.

He also explained that I could earn a reduction in my points if I plead guilty and cooperated with government. The next time I met with Ivey and confirmed all of these things and he agreed. He told me he could probably get me out of CCA if I plead guilty. I needed to discuss this with my wife but I was leaning more and more and wanted to do anything to get out of this hell. She had just got her old job back at Kohls and she said I should do what I thought was right.

I had another bail hearing and was denied bail again due to the Judge not believing I no longer lived in Florida. When I was riding back in the van with chains from head to toe, I decided I was going to plead guilty. I called Ivey the next day and told him I wanted to plead guilty if they let me out.

He set up the hearing within a week and I did it. The Judge agreed to release me pending sentencing. After the hearing I had to go back to CCA to get processed and released. I was one of the first people to ever get bail. My wife and mother in law picked me up that night. It was actually a load off my shoulders to plead guilty. The stress was killing me and I needed to prepare mentally for prison. I was confident I had done the right thing. If I had gone to trial with Ivey I would have lost and gotten more time. I had agreed not just to plead but also to proffer my story for the Government.

I met with them about a month later and in the room were about 4 FBI agents, and IRS agent and the AUSA (Assistant US Attorney). They grilled me for hours and I told them everything I knew. We agreed to meet again in a few weeks and we wound up meeting on two more occasions. They agreed to recommend a 3 point reduction during my sentence.

I was spending as much time as I could with my daughter over the next few months. I was broke so I started selling my watch collection to get some money. I purchased a book on Federal Prisons and remembered that Tony told me to ask to go to Morgantown FCI. He said it was a nice place and I would be happy there.

Happy was not what I expected but what I was reading about the place was good. It took a few months to get our affairs in order and my wife was getting prepared as well. This was going to be hard on her and we were glad she had family around to help her.

I called Inez and told him I wanted to request Morgantown he informed me of my sentencing date. When the date arrived once again I drove myself to the courthouse in Akron. I did not know if I would be held after sentencing or would I be allowed to go home until it was time to report to prison. During the hearing the Judge asked if any of my victims were in the audience.

Of course there were no victims here and he thought that was strange based on my charges. He allowed me to speak and I had been instructed by Ivey on what to say. I barely made it through the speech because I started to cry.

Then it happened, he sentenced me to 8 years and agreed to Morgantown so I could stay close to my family. When he said 8 years it felt like I got punched in the stomach.

I cried all the way home that day. I was told I would get a letter in a week or so with a date to report to Morgantown Federal Prison. Over the next few months we tried to remain positive and strong until it was time to go.

MORGANTOWN FCI

My wife and mother in law drove with me to Morgantown to report to prison. We hugged and cried in the parking lot and I held it together as best I could. I went to the officer sitting in the booth. I told him I was reporting and he told me to have a seat on the wall for a second and he would call someone to help me. I was escorted by another officer to a receiving building where I was told to change clothes. They asked if I had any money with me, and I gave them $1500 dollars which they deposited into my commissary account.

They gave me a pair of pants and a t-shirt and a picture ID which had a number 55200-060. I was told to memorize that number.

An inmate was called and walked me to the medical building where I received a check up and interview. Then we walked across this beautiful campus to my new dorm unit. The campus was cut into a valley with manicured greens and colorful trees and ponds and creeks. I could see several dorm buildings scattered around the campus. I could see a weight lifting area full of guys and a handball court, bocce ball court and volleyball area surrounded by picnic tables.

The first thing I thought was there were no fences anywhere and this placed was clean with sidewalks carved into the grass. In the distance I could see a baseball field with a track around the field and a basketball court near a really big dorm unit.

When we walked in the front door of the dorm unit called Gerard we entered a large room with six flat screen TV's on the wall and guys sitting on benches and chairs watching. I could see guys in another large room playing cards and an officer's station In front but nobody was there. The inmate told me to ask the guys where my room was and he left. He said a corrections officer or CO would be here later to help if I needed anything.

A couple of guys showed me to a big room with four bunk beds and a large table with lockers beside each bed. I was on a top bunk so I made my bed and went back outside. I quickly realized you could come and go as you pleased.

As I walked down the hill toward the campus a speaker announced, RECALL and all of the guys outside started walking toward the units so I assumed we had to return inside. This time I noticed two CO's in the booth and they made an announcement once everyone was inside, Count Time, they said. Everyone headed to there room so I did the same. Seven other guys were in the room standing and they told me it was 4 o'clock count time and I had to stand beside my bunk quietly.
The other inmates had on a gray sweatsuit and some had on a khaki uniform with boots. A CO walked into the room and counted everyone and continued down the hall to other rooms. I could see other rooms only had two inmates in them.

Shortly after another CO came by counting someone clicked the microphone speaker twice and everyone in the room started talking and walking in and out. I introduced myself to my bunkmate a little black guy named Jimmy and he told me it meant count was clear and we had to get ready for dinner in about an hour.

The front of the unit was glass and I could see the campus was empty so I assumed we were not allowed to go outside now and then around 5 o'clock the speaker said Gerard unit and everyone started leaving the unit to go the the cafeteria. It was about a half mile away in a building near the medical building and there were hundreds of inmates in line.

Dinner was not bad, there were about 100 tables of four in this cafeteria. Trays were like in high school and you had a choice of drinks from a machine. After dinner I noticed guys walking in to a big building so I followed and inside was a huge auditorium with about 400 seats and inside a big screen. A movie poster was on the wall so I assumed this was a movie theatre.

Down the hall was a big library. The library was nice there were hundreds of magazines and newspapers from major cities and lots of books. Across from the library was a full gymnasium where guys were playing basketball. A little room in front of the gym was full of equipment.

There were bulletin boards on the walls of the hall listing classes and other activities and around the corner were classrooms wrapped around the building. I walked to another area which opened into a huge room full of pool tables and vending machines lining the wall. There were ping pong tables and in the back was a wall of about 30 computers and chairs and guys were taking turns on the computers.

I continued outside surprised at what I saw this was not what I expected prison to be like. Guys were everywhere on the campus just relaxing or exercising or doing whatever they wanted and there were no CO's visible. I had a seat on a bench and checked out the scenery which was really nice.

This place was surrounded by mountains and the campus was like a park in some areas. Still there were no fences or barb wire anywhere. I decided to walk around and see if I could find Derrick. He was my friend and one of my agents who got 3 years and was sentenced before me. He had been here about 6 months already but I did not know what unit he lived in.

I walked to the front of the campus near a large pond. I could see a big chapel with guys going in and out and then I saw him sitting on a bench talking to another guy by the pond. I walked up and surprised him and asked whats up. He introduced me to the guy he was talking to a young guy named Travis. We talked until it got dark. Derrick said he did not like it here and I told him you have no idea what bad is.

CCA was 100 times worse than this place. I told him this was like paradise compared to CCA. He just did not want to be here even though it was not too bad a place. Derrick had on a khaki uniform which he told me I would get tomorrow.

He showed me the laundry building over by the cafeteria and told me I had to be there early in the morning to get my stuff. Then the speaker announced RECALL and everyone started heading to their units. It was about 9:30 and Derrick said the campus was now closed. So he showed me what unit he lived in which was called Alex Unit. It was the largest unit holding about 400 inmates.

I went back to my room and a couple of inmates were sitting at the table and they started asking me questions. Where are you from? What are you in for? How much time did you get? I had experienced this at CCA so I was used to it. It gave me the opportunity to ask some questions.

They told me that I could go to commissary store tomorrow and get my supplies and some groceries. They told me what to make sure I bought, a radio for the TV's, a sweat suit, gym shorts and sneakers along with any hygiene items I was used to using. As a new person I was allowed to shop twice the first week but after that only once a week. They gave me a commissary list with prices and items and I started to make my list. I was also told that near the front door was a call out sheet and that I needed to make sure I checked it every night because it lists your appointments the next day. I went to look and it had my name with Laundry at 7am but in military time next to it. They explained I would get a bag of stuff and a pillow and that I could not miss that appointment.

There were 4 phones on the wall near the front door so I went to make a call. You had to have money in your account to use the phones and your inmate number was your access. I called my wife to let her know I was ok and that I would call her every other evening. I was told you only get 300 minutes per month so you have to be careful not to run out of minutes. Lights out was 12 o'clock during the week and 2 am on weekends. We had another count at 10 o'clock and then I finished my commissary list and got ready and climbed into bed. Prison is loud because there are so many inmates so you have to learn to sleep with a little noise but it was not bad here after 12 most guys were listening to their radios or sleeping.

Breakfast was served from 6 am to 7 am and I arrived at the laundry building for my appointment. Laundry was run by inmates and everyone was in uniform and they took me into the back of the facility to a room where they helped me try on a uniform to get my right size. They gave me a big mesh bag and 3 sets of the khaki uniforms.

Then they sent me to the shoe area and I picked out my size of black army boots. I was given 5 pair of underwear, socks, and t-shirts and a winter coat and hat.
Then sheets, two blankets, pillow cases and a nice pillow. I left laundry with a huge bag and noticed that the commissary store was next door and guys were already in line.

So I hurried back to my unit, put my stuff away and headed to the store. I knew immediately I could not walk in these army boots and I realized that they were mandatory when you had the uniform on.

Commissary was like a convenient store with everything except fresh food. Each inmate was allowed a maximum of $300 dollar spending limit per month regardless of how much money you had in your account. Only in your first week can you spend more because you have so much to buy. Prison is not cheap. Even though you are given 3 meals per day everything else you may need costs money. With a spending limit of $300 you have to carefully manage your commissary spending and your phone calls.

I spent $250 my first day and another $200 two days later to get things I later realized I needed. Items were not cheap like a sweatsuit was $25, a $30 radio, sneakers were $60 and then snacks, food and personal items and a lock for my locker. I had to buy hangers to hang my uniforms. A watch for $20 dollars and gym shorts at $15 a piece.

At the store, inmates worked there and you turned in your list with the items you wanted checked off and they shopped for you and then you bagged it up with your mesh bag. If the store was out of an item you wanted there were no replacements and if you forgot something you could not add it after you turned in your list. You could only shop once per week and only on your day which was based on your inmate number.

I went back to my unit and put my groceries away and decided to walk around to get familiar with the campus before lunch. There were 7 dorm units spread around the campus. Although this placed had a lot of freedom there were rules. You were not allowed to be in any unit except your assigned unit. If you were visiting some you had to stay outside and have someone get them for you. There was an administration building where the Warden and staff worked along with CO's on duty.

Each dorm had an officer station where CO's would be during count times and in the evenings mostly. Below the administration building was medical which was called Health Services and it included doctors offices, nurses stations, a dentist office, an eye doctor, and a pharmacy. Another building was the captain and lieutenants offices. They ran the prisons operations as well as the SHU or special housing unit. Another building where inmates who violated the rules were housed and disciplined. This was the only building that had barb wire and cells. There was a facilities building which housed all trades like plumbing, electrical, landscaping, etc. Inmates had jobs in all of these trades and operated all equipment.

There was the education and rec department in one building. Next door was a building called Unicore which was a place where inmates worked doing computer work. Unicore was the hardest job to get since it paid the best wage and employed about 100 inmates. It was almost 12 o'clock and announcement was made that the campus was closed. I headed back to my unit to get ready for lunch. When Gerard was called on the speaker we all headed to lunch. I could tell lunch was more formal because everyone had on their uniform and boots, no sweats. The cafeteria was packed with the Warden and other staff in their suits lining the walls and the food was incredible. It was Thursday, chicken day, with mac and cheese, green beans, rolls and cake.
There was a salad bar with veggies. It was obvious that lunch was different from breakfast and dinner, it was special. A typical day in prison was breakfast at 6 to 7am, followed by work call at 7:30.

Everyone had to have a job except new inmates. You were given a week to just get acclimated to the prison and then you had to find a job. From 7:30 to 3:30 was work hours. The campus was more formal during this time you had to be in uniform at all times unless you were off duty and in a recreation area. Then you had a 4 o'clock count and then dinner at 5pm was informal. You could wear sweats and sneakers to dinner and then the campus was open until 9:30pm when you had to return to your dorm unit. TV's were on from 11am to 12pm on weekdays and 6 am until 2am on weekends.

The housing units were large ranch style buildings. My unit was medium size and held 100 inmates. There were 3 types of rooms. An overflow room like I was in that held 8 inmates, a wing which held about 30 inmates and 2 man rooms which were based on seniority. The units had microwaves, hot water lines for tea and coffee and soups, an ice machine numerous bathrooms with real mirrors which was very unusual for a prison. Glass could be used as a weapon so you would never see that except in a place like this.

Each bathroom had individual showers with privacy. Everyone had a plastic chair for the TV room and a locker near the bed. The unit was very clean and cleaned daily by orderlies. That job paid about $30 per month.

Each unit had a unit manager, secretary, and counselor on staff during the day. Work call ws 7:30 am and you had to get up and make your bed even if you did not have to go to work. You could sleep on top of your cover during the day but your area had to be clean and tidy. Inspections were weekly and determined the order for lunch and dinner for the units.

At this prison you had to have no violence in your criminal history in order to be here. You also had to have less than 10 year sentences. There were inmates from all professions as well as small time drug dealers but unlike CCA there did not seemed to be a lot of fighting and no killing like at other prisons. Everyone here knew they were going home one day and everyone knew that if they broke the rules they were going to the SHU and subject to being transferred to another prison.

After a week or so I got my first job. It was called compound 1 and the job was to keep an area of the campus clean during the morning and early afternoon. I had to check in with the CO in charge of compound 1 in the morning and after lunch.

About 100 inmates had this job and that's why the campus was so clean. The job took about 30 minutes to do and paid $5 per month. Over the years I had many different jobs as I learned more and more about the best jobs. Some inmates go to school to get their GED so they don't work during the day. There are all kinds of other classes during the day taught by staff and classes in the evening taught by inmates.

Weekends were very casual, no uniforms unless you were going to the visiting room. Movies played Friday night, and twice on Saturday and Sunday. Religious services were in the Chapel for every type of religion you could imagine.

Activities were endless from basketball and softball leagues to chess and pool tournaments to yoga and stretching classes.

My friend Tony was right, prison was way better than CCA. You had a lot of freedom and had to learn to stay busy doing whatever you wanted to allow you to do your time. It was about finding a routine for each day and trying to stick to that routine as much as possible. You have to adjust to your new life and stop thinking about home.
The secret was to get as comfortable as possible within the rules. This would change overtime as you learned more and more and built more relationships with other inmates.

PRISON LIFE

Respect is big in prison and if you want to live without having problems with other inmates you better learn how to respect each other. My past life as a stockbroker helped me tremendously because I could talk to anybody. Although there were not many fights in Morgantown there were arguments and it was usually over some form of disrespect. It helped in Morgantown that race relations were relaxed. In most prisons different races did not associate but here everybody was cool with each other. TV's are another major issue in prisons. At CCA I saw so many fights over the TV.

In our unit we had six TV's on the wall so during the day 2 TV's were for sports, 1 for news, 2 for miscellaneous and 1 for the Spanish Inmates. During the day it was open rule for changing channels on a first come basis. At night starting at 8 pm a TV schedule was followed based on requests. One inmate was chosen to be in charge of the TV schedule. If you wanted to watch a show you put your request in with him as early as possible and it was his job to make it happen. This system avoided problems and minimized arguments. Our TV room held about 75 guys comfortably and was full most nights.

On weekends inmates cooked with the microwaves. You could buy food from the commissary but if you really like to cook you wanted to have relationships with the guys that worked in the kitchen. They stole food from the kitchen and sold it to inmates in their unit. If you knew a cook you could get the best food like meats and veggies. Guys made amazing meals and pizza's and deserts. Money was not allowed in prison so the money was packs of tuna. These sold for 1 dollar in the commissary so they were used as the currency of the prison.

Visits were important but they were also hard. Morgantown had a very nice visiting room that held about 100 people along with a kids room full of toys.

My wife would bring my daughter once every few months and we would have a good time and then cry when it was time to leave. Visiting hours were Friday evening and Saturday and Sunday all day.There were vending machines in the visiting rooms with microwavable food so you could have lunch with your family. It was nice to have visits but it could make it hard to do time if you have them too often.

After a few weeks there I was learning about a couple of medical passes that I needed to try and get. One was called a soft shoe pass. These boots were killing my feet and they were swollen more and more each day. A soft shoe pass would allow me to buy a soft pair of casual leather shoes and I would not have to wear boots. The other pass was a bottom bunk pass so I would not have to sleep on the top bunk. These passes were had to get and only a doctor could issue them. I used the fact that I was a diabetic and successfully got the passes. I was getting more and more comfortable each day. It took about 6 months to really settle in and stop thinking about outside life.

I enjoyed shooting pool, playing basketball, playing poker and pinochle and taking some classes like yoga and graphic arts. Later I would even teach classes on buying stocks and credit repair. I lived at the movie theatre every week and went to a lot concerts. There were many types of bands and some guys were really talented.

My friend Derrick lived in Alex unit but we spent a lot of time together as much as possible. He would be here for about 2 ½ years so we wanted to hang out while we could. We even had our families come at the same time for visits sometime. Outside of Derrick I mostly spent time with inmates that had similar backgrounds. There were many investment guys here and we tended to congregate.

It was really easy to forget I was in prison in a place like this. When I was locked down 23 hours per day in CCA you knew you were in jail.Here it felt more like some kind of camp except there were no women here except staff. For me it was count time that made me feel like I was in prison.

The CO's counted at 4pm, 10pm and several times overnight while you were sleep. Weekends were so laid back you could actually sleep all weekend if you wanted. I chose to shoot a lot of pool and go to both the early movie and the late movie all weekend if I did not have a visit. I had an 8 year sentence which meant I had to do 78 months which is a long time. So I really had to learn how to do time.

The inmates call it bidding or learning how to bid. I was so busy most days with activities or card games that I was so exhausted at the end of the day that I slept good.

There were also real characters in prison. Some guys were crazy as hell and some guys were really funny. Many of these inmates had some amazing talents. I am normally a quiet guy and I tend to mind my own business but in prison there is no privacy. You are forced to communicate with people of all walks of life. Inmates love to tell stories about their crimes and how they got caught. Every night at bedtime somebody would be talking about their criminal life. Some of these stories were amazing.

The various types of ways that people broke the law would blow your mind. It really was like crime school. I also like to read so I spent a lot time in the library.
We had every popular magazines and newspapers and a great selection of books. We could also request books from a local library.

I read at least two books a week my entire time in prison. My wife would also order me books from Amazon that I wanted. We were doing so much better after the first six months. We had a routine that was working where we talked every other night for like 10 minutes to keep me informed about her life and my daughter's growth until the next visit. I watched her grow from 2 years old to 8 years old in the visiting room. I loved every minute of those visits.

Another issue is bunkmates. Unless you had a 2 man room you do not choose your bunkmates and I had a few during my years. My fist bunkmate was a guy named ponytail, he was a stone cold criminal. He worked in the kitchen and stole everything he could. He also sold cigarettes and hid them in the ceiling in our room. He was crazy as hell but I got along with him ok.

My favorite bunkmate was a guy named Tran. He as a vietnamese guy doing 10 years for growing marijuana. He owned two houses and they were full of marijuana plants until he got caught. Tran was an amazing cook. The things he could cook in a microwave you would not believe. He was also one of the best card players I have ever seen. We lived together for almost 3 years.

My first year was winding down and we were getting close to the holidays. Prison is tough during the holidays and the phones were very busy. Morgantown did a good job during the holidays. First was Thanksgiving and the dinner was amazing. We had so much food it would not fit on the tray. During Christmas we had decorating contest with each unit for special privileges. In Gerard we had a big beautiful tree by the front door. We had concerts and plays in the auditorium and then a special meal on Christmas day. We also had special meals on New Year's and during the Super Bowl we had wings.

THE GOVERNMENT IS BACK

My first year was going well. I was learning more and more each how to do time. I made it through my first holiday without losing my mind and was eager to start the next year. And then I called my wife one day and she told me that I needed to call my step-father Leon because the government was messing with him. It was like a punch in my gut. I really thought things were over. I plead guilty and told them everything why would they bother him other than to mess with me. I called him and he told me the feds with investigating him and his lawyer Steve for securities fraud. My stepfather was one of my clients.

He had pooled together some of his close friends to come up with the $1,000,000 minimum investment. Steve his attorney handled the paperwork for each of his friends. The Government did not care they were charging both of them with soliciting investment money and securities fraud based on my deal. It was the same AUSA that handled my case that was doing this bullshit and I was certain it was done to stick it to me. I had 18 other agents who pooled money and they did nothing to them. My stepfather was pissed and he and Steve were planning to go to trial and fight these charges. This was heavy on my heart for the next couple of months because I felt helpless about it.

Then one day I was walking to my unit after lunch and they called my name on the speaker to report to the back door of R&D. They only called inmates that were leaving to the back door of R&D.

When I got there they told me to go pack my things and put it in storage because I was leaving to go to court. I went to pack and called my attorney who had no idea what was going on. I left the next morning. When you travel with the federal marshals it is very humiliating. You are handcuffed and leg irons are placed on your legs and you are treated like a criminal. I had no idea where I was going and they drove me in a van to the Pittsburgh airport. On the tarmac was the conair jet and inmates were being loaded onto the plane and several buses next to the plane.

There were federal marshals with shotguns posted around the plane. I was scared shitless thinking I was getting on this plane which looked like it could barely fly. Then a marshal came on the bus and said the following names come forward and get on the CCA bus. My name was called and I knew I was headed back to hell.

It was night time when we arrived at CCA and I had to go through the entire processing again. By the time I was taken to a pod and assigned a bed, it was like midnight and I was exhausted. My bunkmate was a little spanish guy from Akron who was in for selling drugs. You never know what you are going to get at CCA but he seemed harmless. I was there for about a week before my attorney showed up to meet me. When I walked in the room the feds were there with him. When I asked what the hell was going on, they told me they brought me here because my stepfather was going to trial and they wanted me to testify against him. I starting laughing and told them they were crazy. I was not scared of these people anymore. I had already spent a almost a year in prison so there was nothing they could do to me.

I told them to listen carefully that if they called me to the stand I would say they had nothing to do with my business other than being a client in other words a victim. They were pissed.

They said they were going to call me to testify anyway and got up and left. I went back to my pod and quickly called my stepfather and told him that I was in Youngstown and that they brought me here to testify at your trial.

The trial was like three weeks away and he was determined to fight these charges. I told him what I was going to say but I could tell he was now scared. It was like he did not believe me. I would never do anything to hurt my stepfather but he felt that regardless my testimony could hurt their case. Meanwhile I had to sit in this hell hole for three weeks and it was just as bad now as it was the first time I was here. I could not wait to get back to Morgantown.

When it came time for the trial nothing happened so I called my wife to find out what was going on and she told me that my stepfather and Steve took a plea deal. Steve got 1 year and my stepfather got 18 months.

The Government just left me in CCA for two months after they pled. I had to have my wife call the Director of Prisons in order to get sent back to Morgantown. I was so tired of the fighting in CCA that by the time I stepped off the bus at Morgantown I wanted to kiss the ground. I was sent back to Gerard unit but I lost my room. I was moved to D-wing with a bottom bunk and no bunkmate. D wing was an open wing of the building that housed about 30 inmates.

I had to try and get my job back but compound 1 was now full so I lost that job. My counselor gave me a job in the Chapel as an orderly. There were six of us cleaning the Chapel which took about 30 minutes. The job sucked because you could not leave you had to sit there all day. I knew I could not stay in this job during my time. After a couple of months I got lucky, Unicore sent for me. I had been on the waitlist for a year and finally got the job. Uniore is the prison industries. Our Unicor did patent editing which was really cool. We worked on actual US patents and we editing them to put them into the format that the Government wanted. It was a7:30-3:30 job and paid about $100 per month. We worked in a really nice air conditioned building with new computers.

Derrick and Travis both worked there so we could hang out. Unicor had special privileges like going to lunch first and going to commissary first. I really enjoyed this job and kept it for the next two years until the contract ended.

One day a guy I knew from Cleveland that knew my family came to my unit looking for me. He told me my stepfather was here in his unit Randolph. I went to the unit and snuck in to see if he was serious. My stepfather was sleep and I woke him and asked what the hell he was doing here. He had been assigned to a medical prison in North Carolina but they decided he was too healthy to stay there so they shipped him to Morgantown. I was glad to see him and we spent time together almost every day.

My stepfather was about 70 years old but he was in good shape for his age. He got a job in Laundry which was where most of the older guys worked. It was great because I could arrange for visits from my two sisters coming to see him with my wife and daughter coming to see me.

After a few months guys were coming to me from Randolph unit telling me my stepfather was going to get his ass kicked because he was bossing people around in the unit. I had to tell him to chill out he was not a lawyer anymore. He was doing 18 months for nothing and it was really telling how bad the Government could be. We talked about it alot but ultimately just decided to deal with it.

My stepfather would give me the best blankets, sheets and pillows from laundry whenever they got new stuff. My bed was like a cloud it was so comfortable. Extra t-shirts and socks you name it he would bring me whatever I wanted. We went to the movies together every weekend and would sit by the pond and talk every night. His 18 months went by so fast and then he was gone home. He died two years later and the prison would not let me go to the funeral because he was not my biological father.

I was settling in to my new bed and roommates in D-wing. I developed some really good friends. T was Goose, a guy from Detroit that owned a mechanic shop and was here on a drug charge. He was a clown and loved to tell jokes and laugh. He would sing Motown songs in the shower and he could actually sing.

There was Sean Caso a stockbroker from Fairmont he was here because he had a gambling problem and started to embezzle his clients money. He eventually called the Government and told on himself and got three years. His bunkmate was a guy named Ace, a drug dealer from Philadelphia. Next to them was big Art. He was like 400 pounds and had a really loud voice. He and I used to argue about nothing all the time and became good friends.

There was Sagg a guy from Saginaw Michigan doing 10 years for selling drugs and his bunkmate Jack from Pittsburgh. Jack was a really crazy guy who loved to laugh. He and Sagg were bunkies for like 5 years. There was Pop, an old Italian guy who was finishing up 10 years of a 20 year sentence for huge quantities of drugs. He was about 70 years old and had spent most of his life in prison. Finally there was a guy named Jay. He was doing his last 6 years of a 24 year sentence. He had worked his way down from some really bad prisons. He was a really cool guy. Out of 30 inmates in the D wing these were the guys I hung out with the most. We all became good friends while doing our time.

Morgantown was getting a reputation in the Federal Prison System as the place to do time. There were famous people coming all the time. During my time there you had guys like Jack the Jeweler from New York. He was the Jeweler to the rap stars and owned a famous store in the diamond district. Republican Congressman Nathan from Ohio was doing three years for accepting bribes. Richard Harrison the winner of the first survivor TV show was doing 3 years for not paying taxes on the prize money he won on the show. John Brunson was a scientist with NASA during the Reagan Administration. He taught a really good class on space travel. I am sure there were others but these few guys I met during my years at Morgantown.

THE HALFWAY POINT

By my third year both Derrick and my stepfather had gone home and I still had 3 ½ years to go. I met a few guys that were fighting there case from prison and I started spending a lot of time in the law library.

We had access to law computers that could access cases so I started to learn more and more about my case. I discovered that my sentence could be argued as excessive for my criminal history. I taught myself how to submit motions and briefs and filed against my attorney for ineffective assistance.

I spent most of the year doing this to no avail. My Judge rejected my arguments and ruled that I accepted my attorney's performance the day I took a plea. I learned a lot about criminal law but it was too late. Had I known what I learned during that year I would have had a sentence of 3 to 5 years instead of 8 years.

My fourth year I started to gamble a lot. I was playing poker almost every night and I was betting on college and pro football.

I did well with both of them and won enough money that I could supplement what my wife was sending me each month. Every unit had a bookie and these guys made a fortune in prison. Tran and Ace ran the poker game and we had a solid group of 10 guys that played. We used old cards that we marked with denominations as the chips. We actually had some decent sized pots in this game considering we were in prison and could not use real money.

I got a new job that year called compound 3 it was the same as my first job except it was on weekends only. It was like 15 minutes on Saturday and Sunday and I made $5 per month. This job allowed me freedom during the week to do what I wanted to do.

My 5th year I started to exercise. I joined a morning class that involved every type of exercise you could think of. We had about 40 guys in the class and we pushed each other hard. I lost 30 pounds that year and tried my best to keep it off. I was voted in charge of the TV's in the unit that year and that was a pain in the ass. My bunkie Tran was happy because he knew he would get to watch his shows.

We eventually split up that year because I decided to move to a two man room and Tran did not want to leave D wing. I had a room alone because I made a deal with my new counselor that I would help him as a greeter for new inmates. I would help a new guy get situated and explain the rules to them. My original counselor was Mr. Black, he was actually killed that year by his wife for having an affair with a staff member. He was a good guy and we were all sorry to lose him. Your counselor is very important in prison. They are the person you go to in order to get things done. They also run your TEAM, which is a meeting you have every quarter with the unit staff. These meetings are designed to evaluate your progress in prison. They also hand down discipline if you had any Shots. A Shot is given if you break any rules and would result in a loss of privileges.

I had a lot of seniority that year because I had been there longer than most. I also started to teach during this year. I taught a class on how to buy stocks that became one of the most popular classes. I taught the CANSLIM system and these guys did really well learning that system. Later I started to teach a class on credit repair. This class also became a favorite class of the inmates. Time was moving really quickly now because I was extremely busy.

By the 6th year I was ready to go home. The hardest time to do is those last few months.

I was still working out each morning and walking 3 miles on the track during the day. When you are about to leave there is a lot of meetings with the unit secretary getting paperwork done. Taking care of things like getting your license and social security card and just basic things that you need when you leave. I actually got to go to the local DMV to get my drivers license. That was really crazy standing there in my prison uniform with everyone staring at me. They tried to make me take the drivers test again at first and the CO was going to let me drive the prison car. Then a supervisor got involved and I did not have to drive. I was shocked when I was packing my stuff how much I had accumulated in 6 years and 8 months.

Most guys mail their stuff home but I chose not to do that because I had so many books that it would have cost me a fortune. My last 30 days I gave up everything. I got a roommate named Nate. He was a guy with tattoos from head to toe and really not the type of guy I would associate with. He asked if he could move in so he could get the room when I left. He was from a really bad prison in Chicago and would tell me horror stories about the killings he witnessed. He had 5 years to go on a 16 year sentence for assault. Amazingly he was a very smart guy who liked to read. He actually read a lot of my books in that last month. My last night I gave my commissary to my friend Jay and I tried my best to get some sleep that night.

I heard my name called at 6:30 that morning and I had a few guys help me carry my boxes down to R&D. When I got there a small group of guys that I knew had gathered to say goodbye. I had met some really good guys in prison and many of them I will never forget. I had completed 78 months and believe it or not I would actually miss this place. This entire nightmare ordeal cost me over 12 years of my life and I still had 6 months of probation to do at home. I lost $500,000 of equity in my home when they took my home and sold my house. I lost 2 million in cash, $200,000 of furniture in an 8000 square foot home and 3 cars. I spent $800,000 in legal fees and the toll it takes on you personally dealing with the power of the federal government. I lost 6 years of time with my wife and daughter. There is nothing more frightening than the United States vs Steve Thorn on all of your paperwork. You really know the power and resources of the Federal Government after this experience.

The ability to take your liberty is a power unlike any you will experience in life. They say everything happens for a reason. I do not know why this happened to me. After 12 years of this ordeal I tried to reflect back on what I did wrong if anything. I am true to myself that my accounting practices were terrible and that I should have paid my taxes on the money I was earning. But I did not commit the crimes I was charged with except for tax evasion and although I had to plead guilty to all of them.

I will never agree that I deserved what happened to me. I am not bitter or hateful about what happened. I really believe that life is about experiences and I had a hell of an experience.

I guess I can only imagine what life would have been like if we had completed that big deal. What life would be like if we were doing many of those kinds of deals per year. I have to admit it brings a smile to my face just to think about what I would be doing and how many people I could help doing deals like that each year.

Yield is the return given from an investment. Chasing the High Yield is a powerful thing and once you get caught in that trap it is hard to let it go.
You can visit the SEC website any day and see hundreds of cases whereby people are being charged for trying to do this business. My advice is to stay away because the Federal Government will punish you if you make a mistake. And that punishment will affect your liberty. It's just not worth it.

The end.

Made in the USA
Middletown, DE
12 September 2024